EXPLORING THE HIDDEN REALITIES OF THE SALES WORK IN THE INFORMAL LABOR MARKET: EXPERIENCES OF EXPLOITATION OF THE SALES GIRLS.

I

DECLARATION

I, the undersigned, hereby declare that the work contained in this thesis titled **"Exploring the Hidden Realities of the Sales Work in the Informal Labor Market: Experiences of Exploitation of the Sales Girls."** is my own original work and that I have not previously in its entirety or in part submitted it at any university for a degree or any other place for publication.

Signature: ....

Date: 07.04.2014

ACKNOWLEDGMENT

I am feeling very pleased to acknowledge my deep sense of gratitude and thanks to Department of Women and Gender Studies, University of Dhaka which gave me approval for this study. This research work would have remained incomplete without the support, good will and assistance that I had received from many people at different stages of my work. At first I would like to thank my supervisor Tania Haque. She was always beside me with her invaluable help and guidance. I benefited enormously from her broad and deep knowledge. My words are insufficient to express my gratefulness to her as her guidance and suggestion accomplish this paper.

I like to thank my family member especially I would like to thank my mother and sisters. Shampa Apu you have always supported me in doing this work. All of your supports have always been the best part in my life.

I would like to thank all the faculty members of the Department of Women and Gender Studies, University of Dhaka for always being so supportive to me and appreciating my works and efforts.

Finally I give special thanks to all those people who participated in this study.

TABLE OF CONTENTS

LIST OF TABLES IN TEXT

LIST OF FIGURES IN TEXT

Figure Description   **Page No.**

LIST OF ACRONYMS

ADB   Asian Development Bank

ILO   International Labour Organization

NGO   Non Government Organization

UN   United Nations

WIEGO   Women in Informal Employment: Globalizing and Organizing

CV   Curriculum vita

LOCALLY USED TERMS

Orna	stole
Hartal	strike
Oi Bal Bety	Hey fucking lady
Osovvo Magi	stupid whore
Purdah	Veil
Eid	Main religious festival for Muslim
Salwar- Kamij	Traditional Bangladeshi dress for women.

Abstract

This research examines the exploitative situation of sales girls in Dhaka, Bangladesh. This study discovers the vulnerable condition of sales girls produced and promotes by the informal labor market. This study unveils the social construction of the identity of the sales girls. Most interestingly sales girls have, too often, been portrayed as one dimensional victim-a group of powerless women under male domination vainly struggling for justice and security in Bangladeshi society. This research explores to challenge the one dimensional meaning of gender power relation. This study explores how the intersection of gender with class, culture, sex, shapes different experiences for different categories women as customers and sales girls in the sales industry. The research critically asses how the sales work create an employment sector for poor women of Bangladesh with high level of injustice, insecurity and exploitation. Here this research explores that gender is not the only factor of discrimination against sales work. Class and norms, becomes a vital factor in this context. Finally this study unveils how in one hand, the informal nature of the sales work perpetuate the exploitation over the sales girls, on the other hand how social values exclude the sales from being a decent labor in the society.

Key words: *Labor exploitation, Informal sector, sales girls.*

1.1 Introduction

This paper is an effort to tell the story of the neglected voice and problems of the sales girls in Bangladesh. In the begging of the study I would therefore like to begin with a direct quote from a respondent:

"One day I was busy with arranging the products with my colleague then a man came and asks for a male beauty product. When I came to him and ask the name the products, he started to describe the secret part of his body. He told about some problem in the lower portion of his body as well as the secret part of men's body. His words were too vulgar. Actually he wanted to make me hear that all slang direction."

Sales industry is a quite new profession for women and it is easily available with good packages. Moreover this is a strong wing of the informal labor market. The deregulation of the informal labor market imposes its labor into a worst exploitation. Women become the worst victim of this exploitative situation. The employers of the informal labor market have the unitary authority and domination over the employees (Chen, 2006). This industry is predominantly ruled by men worker as well as sales men (Dubas, Hershey, 2007). Beside that this profession is a newly growing up profession for Bangladeshi women. In Bangladesh Women from lower middle class family are coming to join this newly raised job field in the informal sector. Higher education is also not essential for this job so it is highly accessible for women. My current research has found this sector with a great gender implication. However societal values do not encourage sales, retail and marketing as profession for women (Khan, 2000). They often do not consider it a respectful profession for women and they seem to suspect such women as "weak characters" because of their interaction with men in this profession. As a direct effect women may feel stigmatized with her employment. Feminist critiques in this respect reveal that sales girls are treated as an object rather than a worker. Sales girls are used as marketing tool to sell the product easily (Mirza, 2002). This research I conducted to reveals the experiences of sales girls. This study tries to explore that, to what extend the informal nature of this profession produces and promotes the exploitative platform for the sales girls.

1

1.2 Statement of the problem

I found sales industry as a core concept of gender and employment that need to discuss from multiple dimension. To know their everyday experiences of vulneraibilities have become the main grounds that pushed this study to be conducted. The sales profession represents the most important function of any company (Day, 2007). Feminist argument refers that sales jobs do not formal training or a college degree (Khan, 2000). Uneducated or less educated women take this profession as a source of income. Being a class based society women from the lower middle class come to join this profession as a source of earning. In that context labor market arrangement, gender inequalities and patriarchal ideologies play an important role. Female labor becomes the worst victim of exploitative labor relation. This exploitative situation is stronger in the informal sector. Like most of the countries in the developing world, Bangladesh economies have sizeable informal sector. Sales profession still consists in the informal sector as well as the sector of labor exploitation. Due to this manner it can be assumed that that there is a link between working in the informal economy and being the victim of labor exploitation (Sarkar, 2007). The link between working in the informal economy and being the victim of high level of labor exploitation is stronger for women than for men (Sarkar, 2007). Informal sector is the strong producer and promoter of labor exploitation and injustice for female workers. Poor and uneducated women are doubly exploited in this situation as well as in the market of informal labor. Women in this patriarchal sex-gender system, has few capacities to exercise their agency and have few capabilities to bargain and protest for any right (Gerhart, Rynes, 1991).Moreover Sales professional retention is becoming one of the most challenging issues in the field of gender and employment. Form the perspective of the capitalism and its expansion it has studied that the owner wants to keep any person who will sell the product in high scale. Recruiting sales girls is one of the direct result of this perception that customer will be attracted by attractive sales girls (Adidam, 2006). Researchers at University of Alberta have proved that attractive and good looking salesgirls do actually boost sales (Joshi, 2007). Business Professor Jennifer Argo, University of Alberta said that if a shirt is selling by a highly attractive sales girl the male customer evaluated the products higher and they're willing to drop more money on it. Additionally the informal nature of the profession excludes the sales girls from formal regulation, laws and policies (Khan, 2000).

Sales works is segmented in the upper level job of the informal sector (Chen, 2006). It has shown that men tend to work in the upper segmented job sector in the informal sector. By contrast women tend to work in the lower level jobs in the informal sector. There is a fundamental difference in female and male work roles and a need for examination of the nature of these socially accepted sex-

2

bound roles. Although no society is without a sex-based division of labor, there is an extraordinary variety of sex typing of occupations across cultures suggesting that the sex typing is not based on unchangeable, genetic, physiological, or psychological differences between the sexes, but is and has been a social construct. Social construction refers than to do the upper segmented work sector such as sales and retail industry. Although women are advancing in the workplace, sexual segregation is still rife and well maintained by their male counterparts (Clutterbrk, Devine, 1987). Due to this manner sales profession create a new dimension in gender and employment field. This study finds this sector as directly gendered. This research has given a serious attention to the fact on less concern among researcher and both government and non-governmental bodies in this category of informal labor force. Due to these realities this study is to reveal the reality and hidden condition of sales girls working in the different shops and showroom of Dhaka city. In this study it will be analyzed how informal sector produces labor exploitation and insecurity among sales girls. For this, it will find out the working profile of sales girls in Dhaka city.

1.3 Background of the study

Since the number of female workers in the informal sector in Bangladesh has gone up considerably, it implies employment opportunities for them in the formal sector have become restricted. In spite that, the numbers of the working women in the informal labor market is increasing. Here the main focus is that these numbers are increasing in the lower segmented work sectors only such domestic work sector, construction labor sector. While in the upper segmented sectors are still dominate by male labor as sales and retail job sector. Due to these realities the main concept in objectives of this research is sales girls. According to American Heritage Dictionary of the English language (2009), Sales girls are the young women whose job is to help customers and sell things in a store. In Bangladesh every year huge numbers of women join this sector. Mostly these women come from the lower middle class families. This study special focuses here the lower-middle class women. In contemporary society lower middle class implies almost the lowest in the social hierarchy. Lower middle class is a term used in academic sociology and in ordinary conversation to describe those employed in lower tier jobs, as measured by skill, education and lower incomes (Scrase, 2003). The world's population of poor is commonly estimated at 1300 million (UNDP, 1996). Women, especially in developing countries, bear an unequal share of the burden of poverty; an off-repeated statement in this respect is that 70 percent of the world's poor are women. Bangladesh remains a poor country with a per capita GNP 210 US $. Naturally the burden of poverty falls heavily on women. Landlessness and extreme poverty creates additional burdens for women in the family. Sales women found this job as a source of income. This is an accessible income generating sector for Bangladeshi women. This could be a new platform for female labor. However this sector is still dominated by male. To understand the problems of the sales profession we have to know the characteristics of this work. If we turn to the main and the core characteristic of this profession it belongs to the informal labor market. Sales working is a separate wing of the informal sector.

This study focuses on the dichotomy between formal and informal employment. It is now widely accepted that such a dichotomy into formal and informal has established. This dichotomy implies that employment in the informal economy is inferior quality compared with formal employment (i.e., no legal minimum wage, no social protection, poor conditions of work, job insecurity, no severance pay, etc. Current information on Informal Employment in Bangladesh by Asian Development Bank (2008) indicates that women constitutes above 91% informal labor force among total number of working women. Recent statistics on sexual composition of employment in Bangladesh is given below.

Table 1:

Formal and Informal Employment by sex Estimates, 2005-06

SEX	TOTAL	PERCENT EMPLOYED IN	
		FORMAL SECTOR	INFORMAL SECTOR
Male	36,079,828	15.40	84.60
Female	11,276,763	8.71	91.29
Total	47,356,591	12.29	87.71

Source: working paper "Informal Employment in Bangladesh" Asian Development Bank. 2008

4

Here figure 1 is also showing the sex estimation of employment sector in Bangladesh in the year of 2008

Figure 1:

Sex estimation of employment sector in Bangladesh in the year of 2005-2006

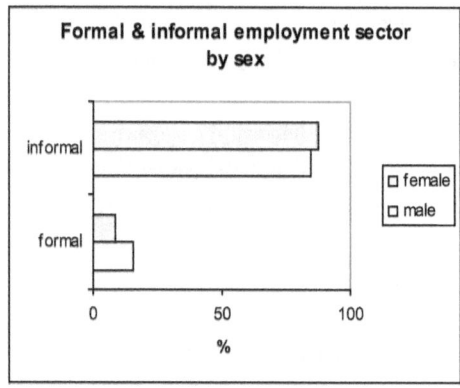

Men outnumber women in the total employed population on a 3:1 ratio. They also dominate over all classes of workers, except in the unpaid worker category, where women are almost double the number of men. Meanwhile, for every male worker in the formal sector there are corresponding 6 male workers in the informal sector. For females, there are lesser opportunities for formal employment such that for every 11 female workers, 10 would be engaged in informal employment compared to one (1) in the formal. Women are very fewer in the sales profession in Bangladesh. Men More than women jump to this profession. It is an upper segmented work sector in the informal labor market. The following statistics proves the sex based job segmentation in the informal sector in Bangladesh.

5

Table 2

Sex based segmentation in the informal sector in Bangladesh

INDUSTRY	FREQUENCY	
	MALE	FEMALE
Agriculture	14,101,835	7,483,906
Fishing	875,830	178,004
Mining and quarrying	38,951	7,095
Manufacturing	2,760,618	908,625
Construction	1,345,488	98,189
Electricity, gas and water	30,487	480
Hotels	564,101	47,969
Financial Intermediation	72,281	22,801
Public Administration	144,594	22,224
Sales, Whole sale and retail trade	5,947,200	390,439
Transport	3,496,282	46,459
Health and social work	102,190	41,077
Other community	1,270,202	328,843
Private household	145,478	616,049
Total	31,243,469	10,294,540

Source: working paper "Informal Employment in Bangladesh" Asian Development Bank. 2008

Table 2 shows that males dominate in all industry types, except in the private household classification. This statistics shows that there are twice as many male informal workers than females in the agriculture sector. Males likewise outnumber females by more than a million workers in the manufacturing, wholesale and retail trade, and transport and communication sectors. Females outnumber males only in the private households with employed persons sector and others. This table shows the little participation of women in the sales industry as well as in the wholesale and retail trade.

In Bangladesh we belong to the patriarchal society. The patriarchal ideologies roots in the household and explores in the public life, in the market. Patriarchal norms force men to jump in the upper class paid employment. By contrast these patriarchal ideologies restrict women to get the economic benefit in the labor market (Charmes, 2000). Especially it become very hard for those women who enter in the male dominated upper segmented job. Due to this manner sales girls faces core hardship after enter in the sales industry. In the patriarchal labor market Sales is still perceived as men's job (Dubas, Hershey 2007). Moreover the informality of the work reinforces the employers to exploit the sales girls. Here the sales girls are doubly exploited first they are a female labor belong to poor family and also they are the labor of informal sector.

1.4 Justification of the study

Sales industry is a growing industry in Bangladesh. Being an agro based country the sales industries mainly growing in the city area. Sales girl is a new concept in the context of Bangladesh. This area was perceived as a men's area. (Dubas, Hershey, 2007). Imaging a sales person always remind us an image of a men figure. Women from lower middle class came to city then join the informal work like sales girls. This sector has become my interest when I found this job is a strong wing of the informal sector. I found this sector is an untouched area in the field of gender and development in Bangladesh. This study will focus to explore the experiences of the sales girls in Dhaka city. Although the present literature recognizes little researches has been conducted to identify the effects of sales persons to selling the products. This review locates the women's roles, rights, and their participation in economic activities. It also focuses on women, marketing and sales industry under the patriarchal system. The next aspect discussed is the sales industries including the problems related to job such as harassment, job hierarchy, sexual division of labor and people's

7

negative attitude towards working women. The problems women face in the labor market at the initial time must stop for integration into the market for labor power. Women are concentrated in unskilled jobs, while skilled jobs are monopolized by men. Ransford (1998) has studied the sexes are widely segregated and management also viewed men and women workers in quite different terms, they appeared to modify their employment strategies to the sex of the workers, not the job performance It is clear that women occupy certain jobs within the workplace including hospitality, personal services, education and health. Moreover Comer (2001) states in his research that traditionally selling positions have been held by men because such jobs have long been regarded as being inherently masculine and women are seen as having no place in the masculine working world. This also refers a man to be a sales person. This perception has forced this study a lot, to know the patriarchal setting in the society as well as in the labor market. There are some gaps in the previous research. To fulfill the gap the current study attempts to explain the interconnection between the social expectation of gender role and the existing job Ghetto in the informal labor market.

Feminist discussion in this field unveiled a new dimension. Objectification of their sexual identity clears the exploitative path of the sales girls. Pratt, Hanson (1995) has studied on a survey conducted to know about the stereotypical observation that women's special characteristics qualify and disqualify them for specific occupations and tasks. In this survey, one of the respondents the boss of a sales representative in an advertising firm asserted "Women in this business do a hell of a lot better than guys do …. Pretty women do better. It's selling the package. If it's a nice package you buy it." This practice is called objectification of sales girls. Above discussed issue opens the discussion about the objectification of women at workplace. According to Jennifer Argo (2001) a product becomes more desirable if an attractive member of the opposite sex is selling it. In the study, researcher found that clothing was rated more desirable if it had been touched or worn by an attractive member of the opposite sex. And some people said they would pay more for the item, even if it hadn't been washed. Jennifer Argo found that if the customer was of average attractiveness, the participant evaluated the shirt negatively. But if a shirt was touched by someone who was highly attractive and of the opposite gender, the customers evaluated the products higher and they were eager to drop more money on it and according to him This results show that it's worth having highly attractive people work there (Agro, 2001). However my study focuses on the strategies of objectification of the sales girls by the employers. This study also examines the factors that give the employers to use and exploit the sales girls.

In the context of women in sales industry under the patriarchal system, in this study the feminist labor market analysts claim that patriarchy is responsible for occupational sex segregation. Hartmann, Mitchell, (1981, 1976; 1974, 1971) found a number of issues determining the reasons for Occupational segregation. Observers have documented a concern that traditionally female-dominated occupations may be valued less than male dominated occupations, therefore female employees receive less pay. Additionally McDowell, Pringle, (1992) indicate that women are clustered in a narrow range of occupations, particularly in the service sector Due to the occupational segregation the sales industry welcomes men rather than women. Khan (2000) has showed here the patriarchal system demotes women to low-paying, women-dominated jobs and if a new profession offers more benefits, only men move into it. However this current research find gap in the previous study. To understand the experiences of the sales girls this research explains the forces of social expected gender role to construct this occupational segregation.

Avila, R (1999) Stated women may be better suited to handle sales positions than their men counterparts; in sales industry it is necessary to be really people oriented, and to have better listening skills and understand the client's wants and needs and women are generally better at this. Women have more potential to become salespeople and can therefore get a marvelous opportunity because of high pay and rapid advancement. However now it has to be finding out the reason why women are not taking it as their career. This study will explain the reason for the less participation of female labor though they have greater skill. Giuffre and Williams (1994) stated that some women sales professionals are sexually harassed in this hetero social; out-of-the-office work settings Women professionals face particular obstacles to career advancement. In this case, these settings produce heterosexual relationships, where customers or colleagues view the saleswomen as potential sexual partners. As a result, women who work in these settings confront problems ranging from gossip to sexual harassment and have to do additional work to avoid this. This study only explained the factors of the sexual harassment of the sales girls rather explaining the consequences of this harassment. This current study will focus to fill this gap and will explain the consequences of the harassment on the sales girls.

Bensiman and Marshall (1997) highlight that feminist analysis of social identity of the labor that draws attention to the "phallic drift" which is manifest in the control of women's identities, Including the identification of women with the private sphere…and men with the public sphere. In the current study the societal construction of sales girls would be discussed. Feminist critique in this manner argues that women's entrance in the male dominate work challenge the gender division of work. The factor of growing insecurity and exploitation among sales girls has become the main

9

objective of the study. The issue of the linkage between the informal labor market and the growing exploitation among the sales girls is unexamined by the previous researchers. My study unveils the reality of informal labor market as a strong producer of injustice and insecurity among the sales girls. At the same time this study uses intersectional analysis to understand the dynamic aspect of gender relation between men- women, women-women. Finally, this study attempts to examine the objectification of women's body in the capitalist patriarchal framework.

1.5 Research objective

This study has given focus on sales girls working in selected showroom and shopping mall in Dhaka city. Over last few decades, there has been a rapid growth in the number of women employed in Bangladesh, with majority of them being engaged in informal sector as sales girl. Where, they experiences high level of injustice and exploitation. This is still perceived as a men's world. The main objective of the study is to find out ways and strategies that perpetuate the exploitative path for the sales girls.

- To understand the social construction of the identity of sales girls.
- To explore customer related experiences and problems of sales girls
- To understand the factors they are been discriminated in comparison to their male colleagues

1.6 Research question

The research question I explore is "What are the strategies or factors that perpetuate the exploitative situation of the sales girls?"

1.7 Methodology and data collection

The experiences and lives of marginalized peoples, as they understand them, provide particularly significant problems to be explained or research agendas' (Harding, 2005). I opt the feminist standpoint theory due to its premises that the evaluation of the dominant institutional practices should be from the standpoint of most marginalized subgroups. Thus, I engaged in this research by taking the standpoint of the marginalized sales girls.

As Sandra Harding notes that standpoint theory 'requires learning to listen attentively to marginalized people; it requires educating oneself about their histories, achievements and performed social relation' (Harding, 2005). My research is focused on sales girls working in different shops and markets of Dhaka city. There are different types of labor working as sales. For this study I have chosen the sales person who sells dress, cosmetics, ornaments, shoes. The research is based on interviews of two sets of people

a) Firstly interview has taken to gather information from sales girls to understand their work environment. This is also to know their thoughts and perception and level of awareness towards the exploitation or injustice in their work.

b) In the second step sexes I have also interviewed sales men know their experiences to work with the sales girl. This is also to compare the basic stand between the sales men and sales girls. Perception of sales men is also examined to understand the factors on which sales girls are discriminated and undervalued.

My research has been conducted on qualitative research technique by focusing on a small sample that I can go in the depth of sales person's lives and thoughts. The qualitative approach was used to gather data from the sales girls because qualitative approach was more appropriate to get detailed data about experiences and problems of sales girls. As qualitative methods are typically flexible, ask mostly "open-ended" questions, participants are free to respond in detail and the relationship between the researcher and the participant is often less formal so it provided great deal of help in gathering precised data from the field. The data has collected through in-depth interviews. Ten in-depth interviews on sales girls and sales men has conducted to explore their working experiences, as Siegle (1990) said In-depth interviewing is an interest in understanding the experience of other people and the meaning they make of that experience . Observation method is also used to get a clear perception of the situation. This method was used to know about the overall environment of that showroom or shop, as Neill (2006) believes that: "In observation, we are generally interested in individual behavior, social behavior, and the material environment" so following this definition this method is easy to get more authentic data and it also provided a clear picture.

I have chosen the area of Dhanmondi and Gulshan in Dhaka to interview the sales girls. Particularly those two areas have been selected as the study place for three reasons. First, this place is situated in a posh area where huge number of shopping mall and showroom are available. Secondly, these two areas are known as the place for shopping as a result sales girls experiences verities of customers. Thirdly I assumed the higher level of social awareness and the NGO involvement in this area will make me easy to interact with the sales men and sales girls. Field visit were carried out over a period of one month. Every participant has assisted with an identification number. Sales girls from the lower middle class household have been selected for the study. The age range of the sales girls is between 22-32 years. Their monthly income is in between 3000-4500 taka. The study is based on both primary and secondary data as newspaper articles and Governmental and Non Governmental Organization (NGOs) reports.

1.8 Practical problems in carrying out proposed research

During conducting this study there were some constrains like

- As a researcher I was not cordially permitted to interview the sales girls.
- There was a big problem as the sales person have very limited time to give interview during their work time.
- Sales girls and sales men tried to avoid answering the sensitive question on sales job.
- Another constrain was sales, girls unwillingness to answer the question on violence and sexual harassment as they are afraid of losing their job.
- Sales girls are afraid to tell anything about the employer of the shop or showroom.
- Time limitation for the research is one of the most serious problems.

CHAPTER TWO: THEORETICAL FRAMEWORK AND FEMINIST STANDPOINT: ARTICULATING THE EXPERIENCES OF SALES GIRLS

To discover the disadvantaged situation as well as the experiences of the sales girls this research will explain the theoretical grounding upon which the study is based. There are several debates among the intellectual on the issue of gender and sales work. The sales work debate also serves to illustrate how different women have different everyday realties and how feminist theories have explained or not explained these differences. It will focus on how feminist perspectives explain the vulnerabilities and injustice experienced by the sales girls in Dhaka city.

2.1 THE INFORMAL ECONOMY, ARENA OF INTERVENTIONS: CONCEPTUAL AND THEORETICAL DEBATES

The recent re-convergence of interest in the informal economy has been accompanied by significant rethinking of the concept. The term informal sector was first initiated by Keith Hart (1970). He describes the informal sector as that part of the urban labor force, which falls outside the organized labor market. In recent years, a group of informed activists and researchers, including members of the global research policy network, Women in Informal Employment: Globalizing and Organizing (WIEGO), have worked with the International Labor Organization (ILO) to broaden the earlier concept and definition of the 'informal sector' to incorporate certain types of informal employment that were not included in the earlier concept and definition (including the official international statistical definition). They seek to include the whole of informality, as it is manifested in industrialized, transition and developing economies and the real world dynamics in labor markets today, particularly the employment arrangements of the working poor. Under this new definition, the informal economy is comprised of all forms of 'informal employment'— that is, employment without labor or social protection—both inside and outside informal enterprises, including both self-employment in small unregistered enterprises and wage employment in unprotected jobs. It describes the key feature of the informal economy as following.

Significance and permanence: The recent re-convergence of interest in the informal economy stems from the recognition that the informal economy is growing; is a permanent, not a short-term,

13

phenomenon; and is a feature of modern capitalist development, not just traditional economies, associated with both growth and global integration.

Segmentation: The informal economy consists of a range of informal enterprises and informal jobs. Yet there are meaningful ways to classify its various segments, as follows:

• Self-employment in informal enterprises: workers in small unregistered or unincorporated enterprises, including:

  o employers
  o own account operators: both heads of family enterprises and single person operators
  o unpaid family workers

• Wage employment in informal jobs: workers without worker benefits or social protection who work for formal or informal firms, for households or with no fixed employer, including:

  o employees of informal enterprises
  o other informal wage workers such as:
    ▪ Casual or day laborers
    ▪ Domestic workers
    ▪ Unregistered or undeclared workers
    ▪ Some temporary or part-time workers
    ▪ Industrial outworkers (also called home workers).

From recent research findings and official data, two stylized global facts emerge about the segmented informal economy. The first fact is that there are significant gaps in earnings within the informal economy: on average, employers have the highest earnings; followed by their employees and other more "regular" informal wage workers; own account operators; "casual" informal wage workers; and industrial outworkers. The second is that, around the world, men tend to be over-represented in the top segment; women tend to be over-represented in the bottom segments; and the shares of men and women in the intermediate segments tend to vary across sectors and countries. These twin facts are depicted graphically in figure.

14

Figure 2:

Segmentation of the informal sector.

Average Earning   **Segmentation by Sex**

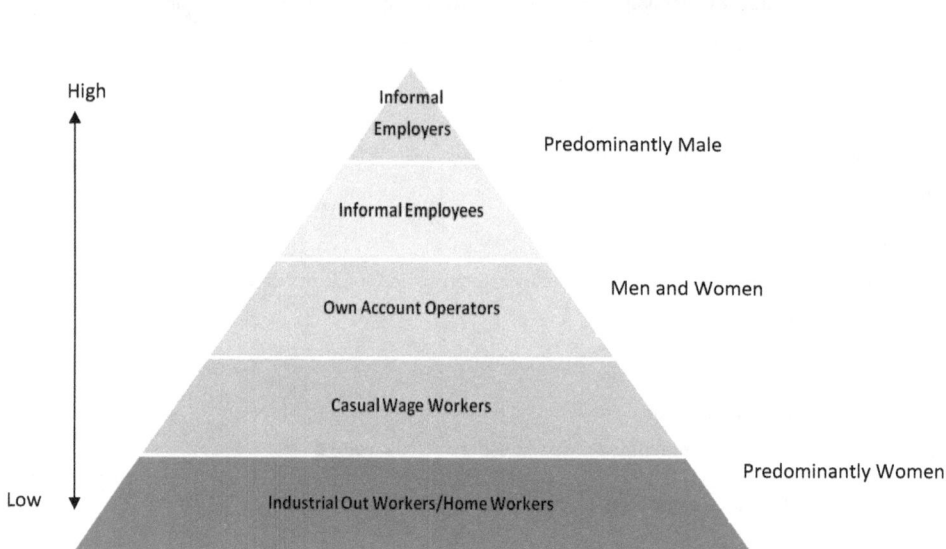

The vast majority of the poor work, but few are able to work their way out of poverty. This is because most of them are engaged in the informal economy, where they are likely to face lower incomes, greater financial risks, lower standards of human development and greater social exclusion compared to better-off workers, especially those who work in the formal economy. The following e framework describes consequences of working in the informal economy. Those who work in the informal economy are likely to have greater deficits in opportunities, rights, protection and voice ... than those who work in the formal economy. However among the working poor in the informal economy, women are more likely than men to be worse off in all of these respects. Chen (2002) describes the dimension of human development in the informal sector.

Income poverty: If one or more members of the household are formally employed, income flows into the household are typically higher (as average wages or earnings are higher in the formal economy than in the informal economy) and expenditure flows out of the household are typically lower (as formal workers have more secure work and

15

greater access to social protection).

Human development gaps: Those who work in the informal economy are less likely than formal workers to have access to social services and more likely to have low levels of health, education and longevity.

Social exclusion: Those who work in the informal economy are more often excluded, than formal workers, from state, market and political institutions that determine the 'rules of the game' in these various spheres.

From the perspective of women and employment this framework views the worst situation of the female labor in Bangladesh. In Bangladesh a recent rise in the fraction of females in total labor force would suggest that the female labor force is growing faster than that of men. It is widely believed that an increasing share of female employment all over the world is not in the formal but in this informal category (Sethuraman, 1998). Increasing rate of participation of females in the labor market is also reflected in the changing sex composition of the total labor force. Which in reality represent a relatively larger proportion of women than men is believed to be in informal employment. In other words there is a gender bias with regard to the incidence of informality. In comparison to men, a large proportion of women not only receives low returns to their labor but is also exposed to vulnerability (Sethuraman, 1998). Additionally the above discussion also shows that informal sector hold a strong segmentation based on gender. Men tend to be consisting in the higher level and women tend to be consisting in the lower level in the structure of the informal labor market.

In analysis of the situation of sales girls feminist have argues that the injustice must be understood as structural rather than cultural (Makeda, 1984). Since sales service is a branch of informal sector. Therefore all the above mentioned oppression and exploitation of informal labor market is more acute for them. The condition of poor women doing sales work places them in a vulnerable position to become the victim of multiple forms of oppression as they are in the informal labor market. Truly their powerlessness is due to the nature and the condition of their work which confines in informal sector. Firstly, their work has no specific regulation and policy. Secondly they do not have any contract paper to claim any complain against the customers, authority and colleagues. Thirdly, the realities sales girls and their experiences to isolation, lack of privacy, lack of option, over dependency on employers. These factors are reinforced by the structure of informal economy. The contract system is a common mode of employment across the occupations studied. How it functions, the modes of recruitment, the incidence of harassment and the engagement of the workers with the state are distinct in different occupations. The complicity of the State in perpetuating these systems of informality has had a crucial and adverse impact on urban poverty. Sales girls are totally excluded from formal contracts paper and documents. The critical concern of this paper has been the exploitation and exclusion of sales girls in the informal sector. The harassment is not visible they face. It is not just harassment; it also limits their bargaining power. It offers precarious employment status, low, irregular or no remuneration, little or no access to social security or protection (Abramo and Valenzuela, 2006).

2.2 SOCIAL EXPECTATION ON A WOMAN AS AN IDEAL WORKER

In the last half-century, women have streamed into the labor force and assumed well-paid professional and managerial positions, but despite such spectacular gains there remains much entrenched gender inequality. Indeed, a great many occupations such as Nurse, teacher, secretary are still hyper segregated "gender ghettos" in which women work almost exclusively with other women, coming into contact with men mainly to serve them. Alongside the female job ghetto there is a large number of male job ghettos. In Occupational Ghettos, Maria Charles and David Grusky (2004) showed that much of this residual occupational segregation is consistent with "gender essentialism," a deeply rooted cultural assumption that women are well-suited to service and nurturance and that men are well-suited to physical labor, technical tasks, and abstract calculation or analysis.

Social expectation theory refers to a body of social theories that are concerned with how our socially received expectations motivate our behavior. Job ghetto is a real example of such expectation. Social expectations play a role in how we perceive and maneuver our social worlds, and an understanding of how our expectations condition us can provide insights into every level of society. Norms provide the basis by which we construct our social expectations. By internalizing gender roles, people learn what kinds of behavior are expected from man-women and adopt a set of expectations for the behavior of others. Stereotypes of gender role such as job ghettos are largely the result of preconceived social expectations. However, whereas the expectations provided by roles are tied to a social function, the expectations that form the basis for stereotypes are largely arbitrary. Society construct it's expectation on the basis of the sexual identity of men and women. Then it creates the job segregation. In this manner job ghetto is constructed to fulfill the social expectation. However, the individuals who have stereotyped expectations projected upon them are not actually obligated to act out those expectations. Thus, people tend to adopt social norms and to tailor their behavior to meet the expectations those norms provide. When others do not meet these expectations, misunderstanding and conflict can result, or it can cause an individual to re-examine his expectations. The model of an ideal worker is being constructed according the social expectation. Further more women are not meeting the expectation are not seen as an ideal one. In the study of Loscocco and Spitze (1991) it has been showed that women in male dominated jobs are less satisfied than women not in male dominated jobs.

Our social values do not expect a woman to work as a sales person (Lawson, 1993). Customers expect to talk with a male sales person rather than a female sales person. Lawson (1993), in her study of car saleswomen, found that some customers responded to women salespersons by simply refusing to deal with them ("Get me a real salesman! What the hell are you doing here?"). Comer (2001) states that traditionally selling positions have been held by men because such jobs have long been regarded as being inherently masculine and women are seen as having no place in the masculine working world but now this shift has been noticeable in the industrial sales forces where women have proved themselves to be very capable salespeople. This study is linked to my research work to understand the reasons of lack of participation of women at sales work and the problems which they face during their job. It is also linked with my objectives of the study of exploring the experiences of the sales girls. That also gives a clear picture to know about the factors that creates these problems.

2.3 POWER RELATION: FROM THE AXES OF SEX AND CLASS EXPLOITATION

In last fifty years, in addition to theorizing about gender relation and inequalities, feminist turn their attention to social theories of power. Power is broadly defined as the ability to influence the outcomes of the events (Sanchez, 1988). It can mean something that an actor posses which is valuable in itself. Powerlessness, in turn, is the lack of influence over circumstances. This work has been inspired by the work of Bell Hooks (1984) thought on the concept that the powerless can also be powerful. Hooks articulated that women lie in the powerless group in the society. At the same time women can be powerful also if it examine from the intersectional lens. The challenges for feminist was to establish a link between gender which proved to be a useful analytical concept for explaining between sexes and powering feminist literature power is often described as top-down. In the gendered power structure, feminist claims male impose power as an attempt to prove them as the dominant authority as women are structurally situated to be dominated in patriarchal system. The traditional definition of power has failed to identify the power relation from multiple axes.

Traditionally power has been defined from two sides. Power relation between men to men, women to women has been given no attention. Power relation has seen from polarized perspective (Dorothy, 1987). This research is sought to address some key analytical concerns to consistently apply a critical perspective which examines situation of sales girls. It is also to examine the gendered relations of power, to develop and apply a more "intersectional" approach which analyses the ways in which gender is (re)produced through its interaction with a range of other axes of social differentiation (such as "race", ethnicity, class, sexuality; age; religion; and ability from a methodological perspective). We speak of women as a group. We must also note that women as a group are not homogenous. Recent feminist debate have explained the theories of power not only as the authority and domination of male because women also a strong agent of patriarchy which is defined as Classic patriarchy. Here women equally impose patriarchal ideologies as well as domination on another woman. Most interestingly sometime it also happens to another male. The cyclical nature of women's power in both public and private sphere and their anticipation of inheriting the authority of upper class women encourage a thorough internalization of this form of patriarchy by the women themselves (Kandiyoti, 2007). From this perspective the experiences of sales girls will direct us to understand the power relation from multidimensional. The existing patriarchal setting not only refers men to dominate women also force upper class women to dominate lower class women. As with earlier discussion of women of the upper class, these relationships shed light on the significance of where one is situated within systems of gender, and economic inequality. Sales girls directly interacts the female customers. They have lot of experience of dealing with female customers. Here the Economical differences alone with the class variation play the most vital role to construct the power relation between two women. However I would say Gender is an operative concept that does not mean only relation between men and women also relation between women and women or men and men. In the sector of sales occupation women are oppressed by multidimensional exploitation. This multidimensional vulnerability comes from the Customers specially the male customers, male colleague and the authority. This domination happened based on sexual identity and class system. Women who are privileged by virtue of their class may dominate over other women who hold subordinate positions within systems of economic inequality. Women may be oppressed by other women. In the context of sales job it become clear that women's group are also capable to exercise power and that women some are more powerful than other (Sanchez, 1995).The issue of exploitation also discloses the multi-dimensional nature of gender and power relation.

2.4 EXAMINING PATRIARCHY AND AGENCY THROUGH AN INTERSECTIONAL LENS

I will operationalize this study in relation to the patriarchal public sphere, which is relevant to the Bangladeshi context As Feldman (2001) defines; patriarchy in Bangladesh is a system of gender relations that determines women's physical and social mobility, rights, access to resources. From the traditional and essential view Patriarchy literally means rule of the father in a male-dominated family. It is thought as a social and ideological construct which considers men (who are the patriarchs) as superior to women. Sylvia Walby in "Theorizing Patriarchy" calls it "a system of social structures and practices in which men dominate, oppress and exploit women" (Walby, 1990). Patriarchy is based on a system of power relations which are hierarchical and unequal where men control women's production, reproduction and sexuality. It imposes masculinity and femininity character stereotypes in society which strengthen the iniquitous power relations between men and women.

However intersectional lens challenge the conventional theory on patriarchy which have articulated women as a homogenous group of oppressed. It challenges the common platform of subjugation of women under male domination (Butler, 1990). The notion of Intersectionality challenges the notions of layers of oppression and discrimination. The discourse of experiences makes Intersectionality, which is one of the indispensable contributions of feminism, to emerge as a significant tool of analysis as well as normative theoretical argument (Hancock, 2007). Mohanty (1991) who criticizes the homogenizing of the 'third world' women by sticking to the patriarchal lens to evaluate their experiences without considering the temporal dimensions.

> 'The notion of a road map of a busy town illustrates the meaning of the Intersectionality of oppression and discrimination. There is Racism Road, Patriarchy Parade, Sexism Street, Colonization Crescent, Religious Persecution Road, and Indigenous Dispossession Highway, Class Street, Caste Street, and so on. The road is full of heavy speeding traffic, and the impact of Intersectionality is when a woman from a marginalized group tries to cross the main intersection. To use this model as an analytical tool, we must unpack each of the 'road names' to explore the origin of the oppressions, and the impact of these on women across a range of situations'' (Bartolomei, 2003).

Theorizing of Intersectionality is the realization that race, color, class, sexuality, nationhood and other social relations of power are equally significant for identities of women, for the process of becoming a woman. Studying on sales job provided the concept of gender and Intersectionality. That refers that patriarchy is not the place of female domination by male. By bringing the intersectional analysis as an approach, the research will focus on the intersection of class, gender, age all of which are power relations to define the experiences of women within the acknowledged gender category. In this study patriarchy is defined as a system where not only men but also women exercise the power. By bringing intersectional lens here women have defined as a category of class and sex. Intersectionality attends segregate identities and move to process of exclusion based on context and dynamics of cross-cutting identities (Davis.K; Forthcoming).

In this study intersection analysis focuses on the direct interaction of men and women as a customers and sales person. This study will analyze how social practices embodied in the intersection of gender, class calls into question that patriarchy as the regular dominant form of social ordering. The main purpose here is to highlight how these differences combine to create women as what Makkonen defined as 'a minority within minority' (2002). Here sales service involves a female-to female and female to male relationship. This relationship consists of upper class female customer and lower-middle class sales girls. It also involves the relation between the upper class female customer and lower-middle class male customer. Sales profession has been a contentious issue for feminist scholars for it demonstrates power differentials among women. Women of the upper class may tolerate gender dominance. However, their class allows them to dominate certain other persons both male and female as sales workers. It challenges essentialist conceptions of gender and universal womanhood since "many women employers simply perpetuate the sexist division of labor by passing on the most devalued work in their lives to another woman-generally a woman of class" (Romero 1992). Yet sales service is also an institution through which gender ideology and sexual inequality operate. This concept suggests that it should be possible to separate the layers out and address the issues one by one. Multiple discriminations based on different grounds at different times, where intersectional discrimination refers to the intersection of discrimination based on several grounds at the same time (Mackinnon, 2002). It does not refuse women's subordination under men's authority. Additionally this study refers sex as not the only factor. Furthermore it says class is equally important factor of patriarchy that provides ability to a woman to dominate another women or men. In this study sales work cross cut both class and sex. Here patriarchy has been viewed from two social-economical grounds. Here, gender and class differences are played out through the subordination of one group of women by another, blurring the fact that both experience subordination within the system of gender inequality.

Agency is also linked with issues of different categories women. Agency is an important aspect of intersectional analysis. The concept of agency is also used to characterize an active and deliberate role for sales girls. In this study intersectional analysis focuses on the interconnection between power and agency. Harre (1984) suggests that when individuals have agency, they conceive of themselves as having the power to decide, to act independently, and to account for their actions. To have agency means that one speaks and acts from a legitimate position that is prior and separable from the particular discourse of interest. Focusing on informality in the context of employment gives a wider role to agency factors, which will prove a more helpful context in which to examine gender issues, and opens a wider policy agenda in extending socio-economic protection to sales girls. Negotiation is a key factor of agency exercise among the labor and employer. The bargaining approach provides a useful framework for the analysis of gender relation. In this manner sales girls stays below in the scale of power relation between employers and customers. Their agency is situated. Women working as sales girl belong to less education with lower social-economic background. These situations take away their capacity to exercise the agency. They fail to bargain for better wage and work condition. Additionally Bing a wing of informal sector sales women do not hold any contract paper or legal documents for recruitment as a sales workers. In that case it is very difficult to organize the workers for the purposes of increasing their bargaining power and it illustrate that having no contract paper it is difficult to claim one employer responsible for protecting workers right (Beneria, 2001). Both class and sex play the game here. For example, here the sales girls are might identify with the high socio-economic status of their employers and customers to draw a line between themselves. More over being a member of female labor force in the informal labor market reinforces their lower agency to bargain for labor right and required, valid work standard.

CHAPTER THREE: EXPLORING THE REALITY OF LABOR EXPLOITATION ON SALES GIRLS

The theoretical framework of the present study demonstrated the insecurity and vulnerabilities of the female labor in the informal sector as sales girls. Social-unacceptance, labor exploitation and objectification, subjugation with financial insecurity are the major hurdles that sales girls face in the informal labor market. The major findings of the research are also presented in terms of these insecurity, exploitation and disadvantages experiencing by the female sales workers in Dhaka

3.1 Presenting data on sales girls

Before going to the main part of the findings, I will briefly discuss some responses stated by sales girls and sales men. Sales industry is a growing up profession in Bangladesh. From a long period this sector was truly occupied by men. Still this job is perceived as a men's profession. Like other countries women in Bangladesh has started to join this profession. Thousands of women are involved in this profession as a sales girl. Still this sector is remaining in the informal economy. However men always hold the upper lined job in the informal sector still now this sector is strongly dominated by men. Bothe the social acceptance and the unregulated arrangement of the sector produces exploitation over the sales girls. Sales girls have stated their exploitative and insecure situation. This research shows this deregulation as the main source of their exploitative situation. Operationalsing the framework developed in chapter 2, I use the following six indicators to investigate the experiences of sales girls.

- Are they socially accepted as sales person?
- Do they experience any exploitation from employers?
- Do they get proper and formal behavior from their customers and employers?
- Are they equally treated as sales men?
- Is it their survival source?
- Do they have job satisfaction?

23

3.2 Sales girl's perception towards their work: Perception of the sales girls on their own profession directly shows their vulnerabilities. Sales girls face challenges every moment. From home to the show room they struggle to survive in this patriarchal market setting. Entrance in a male dominated world is not that much easy for them. They shared their experiences also their perception toward this new sector of female labor. Mili aged 24 said sales work is a good profession for women. This shopping centre is very close to her home. The transportation cost is very minimal for that. Even she said this is also a safe place. She told

> *"This has become like a home for me. Every day I come here and I have to stay the whole day. I am working with four sales men. They are cooperative. Though sometime I feel that some of them are staring at me. I do not give any concentration on that."*
>
> *"I feed my family. I earn for them. However when they knew that I work as a sales girl they oppose it. They forced me to leave the job and to search another job."*

This was the statement of another sales girl named Sathi, aged 23. These cases show that women are taking this profession as challenge. Being a good income generating source sales profession is welcomed by many lower-middle class women. Though there are problems and insecurity but they are trying to survive on it. Another sales girl's name is Shamima. She is a victim of acid crime, stated following

> *"Personally I do not want to build my career in this sector. I had no option. When I will get a better job I will leave this. I do not want to show this face to the customer. They become curious with me. Then I feel shame. I feel that I am an ugly person in this beautiful world. Sales working required good looking but I could not make that requirement. I am afraid off this world"*

This statement shows that still now sales profession demands good looking of the sales girls. Female sexuality is being objectified here. This situation could not be overcome without any formal regulation. The employers of the informal labor have the unitary authority to exploit the employers. Yet the sales profession is in a threaten situation for the sales girls.

3.3 Sales men's perception towards sales girls: Sales men also stated their view on sales work and sales girls. Majed Ali, aged 22 is working as a sales man in Rifles square, Dhanmondi. He thinks sales work is a good profession for men. Women can do batter in swinging the dress rather than to selling the dress. In his word

> *"Sales profession is not suitable for women. People don't like them as a sales person. They can do other job. Garments industry is better for them. People tease them by calling "body selling girls". This is not any respectable profession for women. This is not good for a woman to interact with different kind, different categories person. Our religion has ordered women to stay within the veil. So women should stay away from this type of job"*

This case shows sales men feel that society compare sales girls with character loose person. Public space is traditionally supposed to be a man's space in which a woman has no legitimacy to enter. Traditionally the sales profession is supposed as a men's profession. The societal attitude is very negative towards sales girls because people would think that they are not good women. It was considered that these women have a bad moral character. Moreover this statement also shows that women are supposed to work in the lower level feminine work like swing etc. Another sales men Malik aged 26 said sales men always carry a dominating attitude toward sales girls. This is natural. According to him

> *"Sales girls are very limited in number. They are not confident in this job. Most of the time, they remain in a complexity specially during bargaining with the customer. They are learning the technique of selling here. Sales men are more confident and skilled in this profession. In our shops sales girls works under the supervision of sales men."*

This statement shows that sales men have a dominating attitude toward the sales girls. They do not accept the sales girls equal to them. They feel sales girls are less capable. Hasan Ahmed aged 32, another sales man thinks that sales girls are not skill and educated. However sales girls are highly demanded by the shop owner. According to him there is no chance of harassment. People are not bad at all. He feels that women are harassed because of their own reason. Good girls are not sexually harassed. He told

> *"This is very sad that sales job has become a business for the owner group. They want to hire sale girl rather sales men to sell their products in maximum limit. This is not right. For this reason I think that good women do not come to this profession. There are some kinds of sales girls whom I know are very much provocative. They try to provoke everyone including their colleagues. Those women are raped by their male colleagues. This is not the problem of sales men."*

This statement shows that people even the sales men a strong perception that good women do not want to be a sales girls. Social norms do not allow women to deal the customers in the market place. The perception refers that it may an honorable job for men but not for women. Another sales man named Majed aged 22 believes sales are a good profession. It is also good for women. According to her this profession is not accepted as a women's job. Even society does not give it Recognisation. It is a men's world.

> *"Men are always responsible for harassment; this is not true all time. Sometime sales girls are equally responsible for the harassment. Male customers are not bad. Some kind of sales girls try to get involve with them. Nothing happens from one side. Both parties are involved with this. Women are also responsible for eve tease."*

This case also shows the narrow perception toward the sales girls. Here the matter of women's sexuality and veiling comes directly. Sales girls are thought as an indecent woman before the social restriction.

3.4 Unacceptance of the position of sales girls

The most important focus of this study is the job Ghetto. Society has its own job Ghetto. Women are always forced to care giving activities. From the family to society it is thought as a natural

26

instinct of women to provide care. It has caused the sales profession to be a male dominated job for a long time. Society does not accept women as a labor of this profession.

3.4.1 Unacceptance from family: One of the sales girls named Fahmida, aged 321 stated that firstly her parents were very happy with her new job but after some days some people start to talk about the profession of sales girl. Then her family members become angry with her and start to force her to leave the job. In her words

> *"Especially some of my neighbor said some bad words to my parents. When I joined here my parents were very happy that I have started to earn. This society is not good for all. I always feel that women here are suffering from multidimensional stigma. Where I am earning and helping my family they start to compel me to leave the job. Sometime I feel so frustrated and lonely. I think I could not continue my job. "*

> *"Yes we are challenging the society. We have come here by struggle. Society blames us as a bad woman. I feel sad. My mother says me to do another job. I have told her lies that I have left my job. I had nothing to do. Every day I start my day with a new struggle"*

This was the word from another sales girl named Sathi, aged 23. This cases show women are being stigmatized in this profession. Their families do not accept their profession. They tell lie to their parents. They are struggling every day, every moment. From home to work place they continue their struggle. This is a horrible situation. Their working capability decreases as an effect of this stigmatized situation. This is patriarchy where Social norms restrict women to do work in the male dominating sector. Even Though women are doing well they are not appreciated by the people.

3.4.2 Unacceptance from society: This is the statement of Fatema aged 25. She said

> *"When I return home after whole day labor I feel exhausted and tired. However people from my area talk about men. They gossip on me. Every*

27

day I come out from home with a struggle against my parent then I have
to struggle against the society and work place. I don't think I could take
this profession as my career."

This case shows that society has its own expectation. Gender role is not separate from that. This is the reason that created the gender division of labor. People do not expect a woman to be a sales girl. Women are supposed to care providing work. Here sales girls are directly working in the market environment. People both men and women do not value them as a sales worker. Social norms do not allow women in the male dominated job. Another sales girl named Mili aged 24 feels that some people raise their figure on sales girls. She told

"In my area some of our neighbors think that we do any odd or wrong job.
When I told that I am a sales girl they translate the word "sales" with a
wrong meaning. I know that what they are thinking of me. I have no word
to make them understood. This is my luck that being a working women
being an employed person I am treated very wrongly."

3.5 Experiencing exploitation by the employers

Sales profession is a wing of the informal labor sector. Here the Employers have the highest authority over the sales workers. The sales girls become the worst victim of this ruling authority

3.5.1 Objectification of the sales girls: Mili aged 24, is a sales girl in a renowned showroom of shoe. She said one of the policies of the company is to put sales girl in the men's section. It is thought that sales girls can handle male customer and can maximize the selling. She does not feel comfort in the men's section. She prefers to stay in the ladies section rather handling the gents. She said other sales men remain there but they are forced to that section. In her words

"Though there are many sales men despite that sale girls are given in the
men's section. During the Eid time we had done our duty in men's shoe's
sector, this was very painful. They come and ask us to help them to wear

the shoe. Sometime they try to embarrass us. Sometime we feel very embarrassed to help them to wear the shoe. Some kind of offensive customer makes us harassed. We have nothing to do because in the training period we were trained to fulfill all demand of the customers"

The above case shows that being in the informal sector the sales job do not have any regulation. Moreover the employers take strategy to attract male customers by placing the sales girls in men's section. This is a horrible example of exploitation of sales girls through objectification of their sexuality. Another sales girl named Sathi, aged 23 said that

"The employers want us in an attractive and gorgeous looking. They give more attention on our beauty rather than our capability. Sometime we understand something wrong is happening to us."

Another sales girl named Fatema aged 25 said managers or owners want to recruit sales girl rather than sales men. Maximum rate of the selling is one of the reasons behind of that. She said

"Shop owner feel that sales girl can make people attracted to come to this shop. Then there will be possibilities to sell maximum of the product. They choose fear and good looking girls. Even they prefer unmarried girls rather than married"

These two cases show that sales work is one of the highest places of labor exploitation. Attractive and good looking women are preferred to attract customers. Moreover their strategy shows that unmarried women are more demandable as a sales girl. It shows exclusion from formal rules and regulation allows employers to force the sales girls to do any kind of activities. On the other hand this exclusion from formal laws and regulation also reject the sales girls to use their agency to protest. Here is another sales girl Shamima aged 30 works in a showroom of Twin Tower. She is a victim of acid offence. Her face is burned off acid. She has directly felt the matter of objectification of female sales workers. In this regards she said the following

"I have found this job by Bangladesh Mohila Sonstha. They try to help the acid victim. That is the reason they give me the chance. I had knocked another showroom to get this job. Nobody give me any job. This is for good looking women only. Women are getting more chance because they can increase the selling. Sales girls are the asset of the shop and showroom. I am not beautiful. I am ugly. If you search you will find that no ugly looking women are getting chance"

This above statement directly shows that sales girls are being used to attract customers. Women's body and beauty is being one of the vital factors for the employers. The employers of the informal labor market are free to use the sales girls for any purpose they want. Though the above mentioned sales girl is acid burned she has to suffer a lots as her face is burned. She was refused by many employers. Her burned faces do not attract customers.

3.5.2 Focus on Dressing: In the sales industry employers have the high intention to maximize their profit. Moreover it is a field of informal sector. Labor does not hold any legal support to claim their right. This weakness of the labor group the employers takes the highest chance to dominate them. According to some salesgirls, women are mostly assigned for attraction so that some companies focus on sales girls' dressing. One of the sales girls named Sathi aged 23 said

"Companies focus on our dressing so that people get attracted. Companies force us to wear those dresses which we can't carry easily and we don't feel good. My company force to wear pant shirt which I can't wear freely in our society"

"I covered my head with scarf but my boss said to me, you have not come to perform Hajj or Umrah, on that day I went to washroom and took out it and wept a lot"

This was the word from another sales girl named Pinky. Another sales girl named Mili, aged 24, told about the dress given her as a fixed uniform. She said she has to wear long tops with pant. She does not feel comfort with that. Usually she does not wear pant or tops. But now she is bound to wear this kind of dress. She said

> *"In my home I wear Kamij with Salwar. Every day when I come to my work I have to bring extra dress. I wear Salwar Kamij when I come out from home. I have to bring my uniform in my bag then I change it in the wash room of the market. This brings me in a complexity. I get trouble with it. However I have made this alternative way."*

This case shows that employers another strategy is to give attractive western dresses to attract the customers. Employers force them to wear a western dress which is not our culture. Though Sales girls feel uncomfortable they have to do that. Even sales girls keep it hidden before their family and society. For that they bring that dresses and change it in the washroom of their shopping center.

3.5.3 No contract paper: Sales workers do not hold any contract paper. There is no formal paper as a security of their job. Sathi one of the sales girl, said that she has not signed in any contract paper. She had to face an interview to get the job. She had brought a CV for that. Except CV she does not know about other paper like formal job. She said

> *"I have no contract paper or agreement paper. I get 4000 from this job but I don't know whether it will increase or not. Even I cannot claim for a promotion or increment."*

The above statement shows that contract paper play an important role in every employment. Contract paper can protect labor right. A sales girl can protest any type of violation through her contract paper. In this job of sales girls there is no regulation of contract paper. It gives a space to the employers exploit them.

3.6 Unethical and informal behaviors with the sales girls

Sales girls stated that they do not get formal and decent behavior from both the male and female customers. Their employers also show indecent and informal attitude.

3.6.1 Shouting and using slang word: Pinky aged 22, a sales girl in Rapa Plaza said some customer use slang with them. They try to dominate the sales person to buy the products in fewer prizes. Especially, when they see sales girls they start to shout and use slang word with them. She said

> "One day a big fat and uneducated man come here. He was very rich. He said to show all the dresses. Then I started to show that but he was confused to choose. Then I ask him to decide which one he will take. Then that men start to shout on me. He called me Osovvo Magi (stupid whore). Then he become angry and he leave without taking any dress. Then my supervisor had shouted on me as he felt it was my mistake. "

Another sales girl named Shamima said sometime they meet harsh customer. According to her view they underestimate sales girl where on the other hand they behave with manner with the sales men. She thinks that sales men are strong and they don't bother customer's indecent behavior. For that reason customer choose sales girl to manage anything.

> "Female customers also think that as a sales girl I will negotiate with them. They also underestimate the sales girls. They also use slang. Some of them shout on us. One day a woman come and asked to change her product which she had brought about three month ago. Then I refuse her. Then she started to shout. She called Oi Bal Bety (Hey Fucking Lady) then she forced me to change it. "

The above cases show that female customers also under estimate the sales girls. They often shout on the sales girls. Female customers also believe that sales girls are women and they are inferior. This is a social reality that a woman also dominates another woman under the classic patriarchy. Her socio-economic class allows her to dominate the under leveled sales girls.

3.6.2 Gazing of male customers: Sales girls expressed that mostly men continuously stare them. Just because of this attitude sales girls often get conscious about their dresses and especially for their stoles (Orna) as a result they cannot do their work properly. One of the sales girls named Pinky aged 22 said that she looks after the kids section. Most interestingly she is also in charge of female under garments section. She said that

> *"First men stare us up to down (head to foot) and then they talk to us. I am the only girl here. I have to maintain the kid's products and ladies under garments. I feel very shame. In front of my male collogues I have to deal my customer and have to talk about the under garments. I have to introduce new products also. I feel very nervous when male customer ask me about the under garments. Male customers spontaneously ask me about those. They ask about the size, color and design of ladies under garments. I have observed it for many times that my colleagues enjoy that harassment."*

The above statement shows that sales girls have to become the victim of the harassment of the male customers. Sales girls are trained to satisfy their customers. Any complain from the customer side can demolish the job. Leaving out of formal regulation has become a strong source of abuse of sales girls here. Another sales girl named Saila, aged 25 said sometime she thinks to leave this job. Again she thought about her study and money and decided to continue the job. In her words

> *"Most of the time especially in the evening time some customer come to get round the shopping centers. They don't buy anything. Even they have to intension to buy. Most of them are male customer. They come here and when they see any sales girl they try to talk with them. Sometime they try*

to tease us. I am in charge of kids dresses but they ask me about male products."

"Selling is a business of creating relation with the consumer and costumer. My job is depending on that how much I can sell the products. When I manage the male sector I fell suffocated. Most of the time, they behave very indecently. Sometime they shout on us, sometime they gaze on us. You know we have a fixed uniform here. This is decided by the authority. Sometime male customer comments on our dresses and etc. we don't fell well that time. "

This was the statement from another sales girl named Fatema, aged 25. This case shows that women feel suffocated but cannot protest against the customers. Even if they are directly teased of harassed they can do nothing. Another girl named Laila, aged 25 thinks the most difficult part of her job is to face the male customer. She keep silent since do has the fear to lose her job. She told that

"Harassment from the male customer makes us unwilling to continue the job. However we are bound sometime as we cannot give any complain on any customer to the authority or owner. I have fear to lose my job for this occurrence. For that reason I remain silent and quite to protect my job here."

3.7 Unequal treatments than sales man

The incident of gender division of labor is commonly observed in the sales job. Naturally Women are placed to labor intensive job. Employers have an intention that women are better in handling the customers. That is the reason men are placed in the cash related activities.

3.7.1 Excludes from intellectual activities: One of the girls named Lucky aged 29 said that

> *"There are five positions in cash counter. All of them are male. Not for a single time any women that means sales girls are placed in that position. Our authority does not feel that sales girls can do that batter then a man."*

Another sales girl named Fatema said that they work equally but she gets less than the sales men. Being an expert they are not given that chance. Only sales men can handle the cash counter. Employers think sales girls can better in customer handling rather than cash counter.

3.7.2 Complexity with the male colleagues: Fahmida aged 31, works in a showroom of dresses and cosmetics. Among the six sales people she is the only sales girl. Rests are sales men. She feels isolated from them. Among all male collogues some time she feels very nervous and confused. Another sales girl named Saila aged 25, said about her working experience. Among the problem she thinks she faced problem from her male colleagues in the shop. She thinks male collogues are good but in the sales industry girls are not secured. She also told that

> *"This is secret and shameful that my male colleagues are not safe all time. I am an unmarried woman. My family does not want me as a sales girl. One of the main reasons behind that is male collogues. One day there was a problem in the city on coming Hartal. One of my male collogues ask me to go to home with him as the road was not secured that day. That night was a horrible experience for me. That men was actually more insecure then the road at night."*

The above statement shows that sales girls are always in a stigma and fear about their male colleagues. There are many occurrences of harassment by male colleagues in the work place. Sales profession is not separate from that. Here all the sales workers have to stay the whole day together. The employers have no responsibility towards this insecurity of their labor. There is no labor law. Absence of legal provision creates the platform of high level of insecurity and injustice towards the female labor of sales job.

3.8 Survival source: Many said that they are working here because of their economic condition because there is no other earner in their home. One of the sales girls named Pinky said

> *"Now I need money. I have to support my family. My brother has got married. Now he is not supporting my parents. This is our only income source. Life has become very tough for me."*

This case shows that for that sales girl this is the survival source of the family. Another sales girl named pinky, works in a shopping mall in Dhanmondi. She is working here from one year. She said

> *"I am a student and I have to bear my own expense. My family is not capable to bear that. They have sent me in the job life but now they have lots of problem with my work as I am a sales girl. Sales work is a good profession. I came here by my own choice. I wanted to continue my study. Then I decided to work here."*

The above statement shows that women especially who is studying can do the job of sales. However the continuous deregulation and insecurity of this sector makes women unwilling to work here. It is the truth that women have a lot of opportunity in this sector. Both economically and socially it may be one of the best professions for women.

3.9 No job satisfaction: This is very clear that the existing deregulation and patriarchal market mechanism decreases the natural satisfaction level among the sales girls. Most of the sales girls said they are losing job satisfaction day by day. Along with the Employers dirty policies and informal mechanism of the sales profession limit the capability of the sales girls. These results the decreeing level of job satisfaction. Saila aged 25 states following.

> *"Here I have no job satisfaction. I do not like this job. Now I am managing it somehow. I manage my family and society. Then I have to manage the authority. Somehow I manage to stay away from that odd job. I know that is also my job."*

The present finding locates the women's roles, rights, and their participation in economic activities. It also focuses on women, marketing and sales industry under the patriarchal system. It confirms the insecurity in the patriarchal settings of the sales profession including the problems related to job such as harassment, objectification, job hierarchy, sexual division of labor and people's negative attitude towards the sales women. In this sector women are not welcomed at all. Here the most vital factor is the patriarchal intervention in the labor market. Patriarchy creates the root basement of the exploitation of the sales girls. Interestingly the patriarchal market setting plays the dual role. Firstly the empirical data shows that, the informal nature of the sales profession imposes the sales girls to be objectified by the employers and customers. Secondly data proves societal unacceptance of position of the sales girl as a decent position. The segmentation of informal works shows that in the upper level work such as wage workers and own account workers are always dominated by men. Women are not perceived in this position (Sethuraman, 1998). When sales girls are getting involve in this upper level informal work they are treating as bad women, indecent labor. These two factors has become the core platform of exploitation of the sales girls in this study.

This chapter mainly indicates how the informal nature of this profession along with the patriarchal social setting exploits the professional position of the sales girls. It is clear that sales profession is places in the informal sector. This is the sector where employers and employees are not restricted by any legal system. This exclusion from the formal regulation snatches the capacity to exercise agency to claim any demand or to protest any offence. This deregulation also gives a unitary authority to the employers to use and exploit the sales girls. This study also focuses that in the informal labor market women are not accepted in the upper level as well as those work directly linked with market place. This perception rules on the mind of the people that results to think the sales work as a men's profession. Job segregation is a valuable factor regarding this issue. Entrance of women in the sales industry breaks the pervious believe that said sales as a men's work. It is not only the pressure of norms which weakens women's commitment to work in this sector; it is also the inequality and vulnerability they have to face in this new sector of women, s employment (Heath, 2007). The empirical findings show that, the intersection between sex and class ensures the exploitation in different way. Here lower class women are oppressed by the higher class women. Here class plays the most interesting game. The informal nature of their work reinforces the exploitation and their class reinforces the lower agency. For that reason I found the sales service as a sector where the agency of the sales girls is not only situated but also exploited.

By considering the above cases, we can claim in Bangladesh sales profession is a struggling and challenging profession for women. Being in the informal labor market this sector promotes huge labor exploitation among the female labor specially. Material dependency explores that sales girls become the worst victim of patriarchal labor market setting. It also shows rather than the sales men the Sales girls experience vulnerabilities, injustices, insecurities produced by the various exploitative ways promoted by this sector. The explanation of various factors of sales profession as well as sales service will address the main research question, that is, "what are the strategies or factors that perpetuate the exploitative situation of the sales girls?"

3.10 Intersectionality and the different experiences of the sales girls:

On the basis of above case studies this study has found that sales profession is almost a growing up filed for female labor in Bangladesh. However Sales is a profession which does not need a high level of education or time intensive training however, women are reluctant to join this profession because sales is one of those professions that are socially stigmatized for women and considered less respectable. Except that it is a sector of informal labor market. That promotes and produces high level of injustice and exploitation for the sales girls working here. The factors associate with the reason of exploitation is multi faced. Applying intersectional approach it has came out that sales profession is a section where gender is (re) produced through its interaction with a range of other axes of social differentiation such as class, language, sexuality. By applying the intersectional lens this study has identified seven factors which make them more vulnerable.

3.11 Gender: as an intersectional factor of social relation

In the context of women in sales industry under the patriarchal system, in this study the feminist labor market analysts claim that patriarchy is responsible for occupational sex segregation. Gender inequality is a salient feature in different aspects of Bangladesh, and it is considered as critical factor in labor market. By applying the intersectional lens this study has indentified gender as an axis of discrimination. The patriarchal system demotes women to low-paying, women-dominated jobs and if a new profession offers more benefits, only men move into it. Sales profession may be the best example of it. However when women are hired into predominately men's jobs, gender stereotypes May obvious themselves in workplace cultures that exclude and isolate women (Antilla, 1995; Catalyst, 1995; Kanterand Stein, 1979). Due to this manner this studies shows sales men isolate the sales girls by saying they are entering in the men's job. Societal belief explores that ideal women do not work here. Even there is a difference in gender wise attitude of customers towards the sales girls. It is explored that usually men and women both show harsh attitude but men mostly irritate the sales girls because they stare at them and also pass comments on their figure and dress.

3.12 Sexuality as an intersectional factor of social relation

Sexuality has become a vital factor of exploitation over the sales girls. By using the intersectional lens this study has found two dimensional factor of exploitation. In one hand the above cases show the objectification of female body and beauty. Employer's high demand on good looking and attractive sales girls explores their capitalist nature to maximize the profit. Female sexuality is directly exploited to attract customers in the showrooms. In this case, these settings produce heterosexual relationships between men and women, where male customers or male colleagues view the saleswomen as potential sexual partners. On the other hand it produces the exploitation between homosexual relationships, where the female customers view the sales girls in an inferior level than hers.

3.13 Social Class: intersectional factor of social relation

Another important factor I have found that in the domestic service the social class plays an important role. This study shows that in the shops or showroom the direct interaction of two women

39

may see. One is the female customer another is the sales girl herself. Above cases shows here two women remain in a face to face relation. From the intersectional analysis this research explores that here the power relation exist between the same sexes. Here their sex is same but their class is not same. The customer is the upper class women while the employee is from the lower or middle class background. Here the one woman can dominate another woman because class allows the customer to stay in the higher position. It perceives that sales girls are under the authority of uppers class female customers. Hence In the first barging table the sales girl fails to raise her agency if any unwanted situation comes.

3.14 Classic patriarchy: as an intersectional factor of social relation

Intersectional tool has given this study a different dimension through which this study challenges the tradition meaning of gender. It had assumed that gender is the relation between men and women. Due to this the patriarchy was assumed as the rule of the father where male dominate women though this study shows that in the patriarchy not only men also women dominate women. That is said the "classic patriarchy", where women exercise her power on another women. From the above cases it has become clear that Social identity and class give a woman to dominate another woman. It has already shows that the social identity of a sales girl is nor respectable. Sometime it becomes inferior identity of a woman. By Contrast an upper class woman carry a valuable social identity. That allows her to show her value before the sales girls. It also gives her chance to force and shout on the sales girls in any issue. The whole social setting has produced this inferiority to the sales girls. Not only men also the women dominate tease and criticize the sales girls.

3.15 Cultural Norms: as an intersectional factor of social relation

Through the intersectional analysis this study has given focus on societal-cultural norms on sales girls. In many countries sales girls are treated respectfully. However in Bangladesh our culture societal norm appreciates the sales men as well as their economical involvement in this sector. Whereas the sales girls are think as unethical labor. It is not perceived as respectable profession for women. this is all because of our societal gender division of labor which focuses that women should come in women 's specific fields such as teaching and nursing etc, if a woman joins other profession, then she faces very negative attitude from society.

3.16 Language: as an intersectional factor of social relation

In this research it has identified language as an axis of subordination. One can be dominated by language as well as by the way of approaching. Cases show that sales girls are verbally abused by foul languages. Sales girls are treated by abusive language. Some time customers along with the employers shout on them. Some cases show that sales girls have become habituated with the slang language and word thrown by the customer specially. This situation pushes them in an inferior and subordinated position.

3.17 Sexuality: as an axis of violence

By using the intersectional lens this study shows the occurrence of harassment and abuse as a core factor of exploitation against the sales girls. According to my view point, staring is a part of the visual sexual harassment and it is immensely disturbing for a woman's mental health. This strategy is used by men to keep women out of the public sector. Sales girls become the victim of male Gazing. Cases show that male customers pass comments and slang word on their figure and dresses. They try to interact with the sales girl unusually. Customers harass the sales girls by teasing them. These results directly to the mentality of the sales girls, sometime they want to leave the job. Even they said they do not have any job satisfaction. Considering the above discussion this study explains the intersectional factors behind this exploitative situation that creates the basic differences between the sales men and the sales girls. To understand this exploitative situation this study illustrates the following structure shows on which intersectional factors sales girls are being exploited.

Figure 3. the factors Structure showing of exploitation on sales girls.

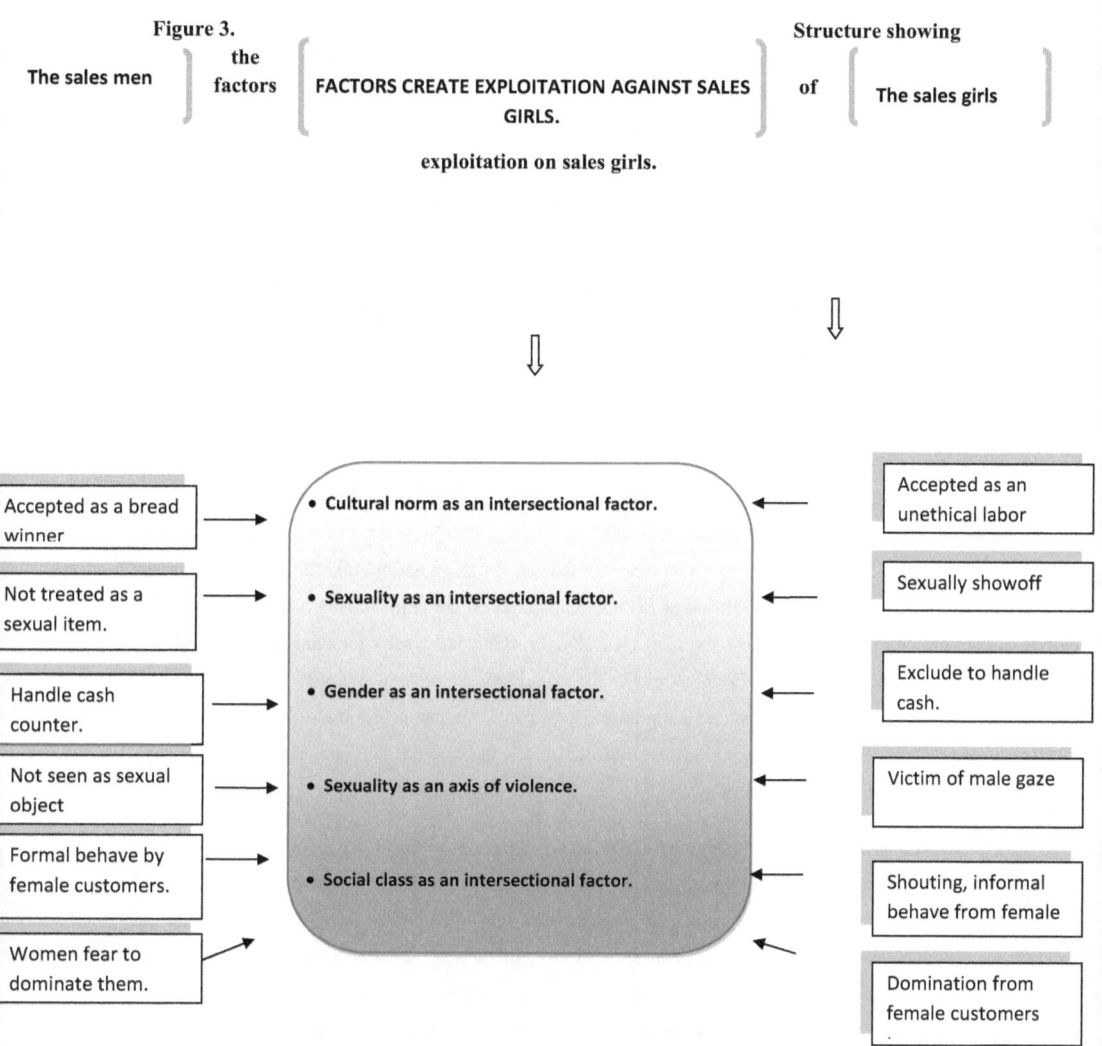

FACTORS CREATE EXPLOITATION AGAINST SALES GIRLS.

The sales men

The sales girls

Accepted as a bread winner

Not treated as a sexual item.

Handle cash counter.

Not seen as sexual object

Formal behave by female customers.

Women fear to dominate them.

• Cultural norm as an intersectional factor.

• Sexuality as an intersectional factor.

• Gender as an intersectional factor.

• Sexuality as an axis of violence.

• Social class as an intersectional factor.

Accepted as an unethical labor

Sexually showoff

Exclude to handle cash.

Victim of male gaze

Shouting, informal behave from female

Domination from female customers .

3.18 Perpetuating the exploitation on women in the sales profession

42

This study has found the sales profession as potential profession for women. However the present situation is just contrast of that. Currently this sector is being the source of higher level of exploitation to the sales girls. This is still a wing of the informal labor market. Informal labors market itself a producer of higher level of insecurity for the female labor. Although the segmentation level of the informal labor market refers that it is much more secured for the upper segmented labor like wage employee, own account employee. In this manner sales job consist in the upper segmented work in the in formal labor market. Due to this study shows that previous studies have claimed that women are always forced in the insecure job in the informal sector (Sethuraman, 1998). Men move to the higher income works in contrast women are forced to join the lower waged job in the informal sector. Traditionally, in Bangladesh women have been viewed as child-bearers and keepers of the home (Wright, 1990). This norm is still unchanged. The labor segmentation placed women in the less waged and less secured job. While men get the higher level secured job (Ransford, 1998). In this manner women are always forced to the feminine job that they do at their home such as cooking, cleaning or caring. This study focuses that when women start to getting involved in the higher level skilled job they are always unwelcomed by the society. From a long time the sales job was dominated by men (Dubas, Hershy, 2007). When women start to join this sector they are said as unethical labor, indecent women. In Bangladesh Huge numbers of women are coming to this profession. However our societal values do not expect that a woman will have a direct link to the market place as the sales girls have. In Bangladesh sales girls are being victimized from two sides. Firstly the informal nature of their work gives a unitary authority to the employers to rule over them. Secondly societal norms exclude them to enter in the male dominated sector. These realities reinforce the exploitation on the sales girls in Bangladesh. . However, I want to flag here four sets of relevant findings.

A. The Informal nature of this sector produces and promotes the strategies of exploitation and vulnerabilities for the sales girls compare to males. The informal characteristics of this profession exclude the sales girls to claim any right in the work place. They are placed in the insecure labor marker. Where there is no regulation to complain against any employers, customers or colleagues. Their agency is not just situated also exploited here. They may the victim of tease, harassment, abuses. However they cannot claim any legal support for that. Because they are the labor of the informal labor market. Their employers have the unitary authority over them to use, exploit or objectify their sexuality.

B. Most interestingly I found this sector of female labor which is totally unwelcomed by our society. The notion of the society is very negative towards this job for women. People try to restrict sales girls to continue her job. This is supposed as an odd job for women. The existing values refers that to deal the customers is men's duty not women's. Women who are working as a sales girl are perceived as unethical, dishonest and immoral women in the society. Sales girl's identity is constructed by the society that is not respectful. Society encourages only men in this position.

C. This study shows the profession of sales work as a vicious cycle of insecurity for the sales girls. Women from lower middle class families come to join this profession. Depravation and exclusion of basic economic benefit pressure them to find any earning source. To overcome this deprivation and exclusion this women take the sales job as a tool to overcome the previous insecurity of their life. However, this inclusion in the sales job in the informal labor market re-excludes them to gain basic justice and security. With high level of exploitation from employer side, customer side and colleague side makes them more vulnerable and insecure. Moreover the informal nature of their job snatches their capacity to exercise their agency.

D. This study challenges the traditional meaning of gender perspective of power. Through the intersectional analysis this study focuses on the multi dimension of gendered power relation. Where gendered power relation was seen as a relation between men and women (Dorthy, 1987). In this study gender and power challenge the homogenous power relation. It shows the power relation of the female customers and sales men. It also shows the power relation between the sales girls and female customers. Under the patriarchal setting an upper class women also dominate the comparatively lower class women. Patriarchy is not the heterosexual power domination of men and women. In this study the Classic patriarchy explores the power relation of two women.

CHAPTER FOUR

4.1 EXPLORING THE HIDDEN REALITY OF URBAN INFORMAL LABOR MARKET

Worldwide there is a growth in the numbers of women working in the informal economy: either as self-employed in unregistered enterprises or as wage workers in unprotected jobs. Despite earlier predictions to the contrary, it is now widely recognized that the informal economy is a permanent phenomenon as source of employment of Bangladeshi women, integrally linked to modern capitalist development and to global integration. In Bangladesh this picture is more acute in the sector of sales profession. Regular deregulation with high level of exploitation over the sales girls claims its capitalist development tendency. This study explores that informal employment is a feature of modern capitalist development, not just a residual feature of traditional economies. Huge number of Women are joining this profession largely however the human development perspective explores the high level of injustice including objectification of women, body, visual and verbal harassment. Many policy-makers, labor advocates and researchers have studied on labor legislation or social protection. However this study focuses in the renewed interest on the sales girls of the informal economy. This is the high time for the policy makers of Bangladesh to turn their eyes on this vulnerable work sector for women. However, the following guiding principles should be seen as essential aspects of a positive policy process to promote and protect sales girls from their exploitative situation.

- First of all policy maker should rethink the informal economy to linkage with the formal economy. They should think to formalize the informal sector. Policymakers have tended to over react to the informal economy, trying to discourage it altogether, to treat it as a social problem or to promote it as a solution to economic stagnation or employment creation. It should rethink by the policy maker that informal economy is the oft-repeated and greatly-misunderstood question of whether or not to 'formalize' the informal economy.

- Sexual Harassment Act has been passed in Bangladesh however its implementation and use as a tool for the protection of salesgirls leave much to be desired. In Bangladesh, there is lack of appropriate platform to understand and address the problems of sales women.

This topic should be taken as a agenda of national issue so that the conditions and problems can come forth.

- There is an immediate need of a regulatory for the workers of informal sector. An appropriate regulation can take the workers out of this exploitative situation. In the question of sales girls there should be a strong regulation for both the employer and employee. There should be a contract paper for the recruitment of sales workers. Where the salary structure, work structure would be mentioned.

- National level intervention is needed to hire women at large number on the management level so that they can understand the problems of salesgirls. It seems that very few women are hired in management, mostly there is only one woman in the masculine culture of management, so management does not give much importance to her single voice and decisions, she feels alienated and cannot take the decisions on her own for the betterment of sales girls. Women should be encouraged to come in this profession at large, so that the societal stigmas attached to this profession can be diminished. For this public and private, both sectors should play a role to aware the people.

- There should be a safe guard of policies and regulation to secure rights of the sales girls.
    o Informal wage workers like sales girls, through extending the scope of existing legislation, promoting collective bargaining agreements and enforcing labor standards.
    o Through which they can build and recognize the 'voice': by joining trade unions, cooperatives, or other membership-based organizations and their representation in relevant policymaking or rule-setting institutions or in collective bargaining agreements.
    o Through the safe guard they can claim any right during harassment and abuses by customers, employers or colleagues.

- Concern body should be more gender sensitive. In most regions of the world, within the informal economy, women tend to be concentrated in lower-return segments than men. As a result, even within the informal economy, there is a significant gender gap in earnings and in the benefits and protection afforded by work. This issue must be addressed by the concern body.

- Finally, to ensure that appropriate policies are put in place, the informal workforce needs to be visible to policymakers. Also, to ensure that the policy approach is well-informed it needs to be evidence-based. Yet there are currently limited data on the informal economy. As During this research I also recognize that there are limited data on the sales workers. Especially in this sector there is a gap in gender disaggregate data. Greater priority needs to be given to the collection of data on sales girls, which is a relatively new topic in labor statistics.

4.2 RESHAPING THE STRATEGIES THROUGH THE SOCIAL JUSTICE DISCOURSE: TRANSFORMATION OF SOCIO- INSTITUTIONAL ARRANGEMENT.

This research explores the circumstances and explains the dilemmas of sales girls working in Dhaka, Bangladesh. Now these days the women in Bangladesh are involving them in this profession. This is a growing sector for women. From a long period of time men had dominated this sector. Still now in Bangladesh the societal norms exclude women to work as a sales girl. This particular service belongs to the informal sector, and is such away from development benefit. Women with little options of choice come to this profession. These women suffer a set of human deprivation in this profession. This study shows the vicious cycle of injustice among the life of the sales girls. Sales girls come from lower-middle class families. Exclusion from economical benefit most of the sales girls chose to work in the sales sector. Here By the unbarring economical deprivation they come to search for an earning source to survive. To overcome the injustice they involve them self in the sales work. This inclusion in the informal sector as a sales girl provides them a more exploitative platform and space to survive. Along with harassment, tease they experience high level of injustice by the employers through objectification of their sexuality and body to attract customers. This exploitation re-exclude them form the natural job satisfaction. These sets of exploitations reproduce a new injustice in their life. The informal nature of their work also re-excludes them to exercise their agency and decision making power. Before joining in the sales work these poor women view it as an employment that can take them out of poverty and insecurity. That, in reality re-include in injustice and insecurity with high level of exploitation. Ultimately in this context sales profession is shifting the risk of insecurity among the sales women. This is resulting that maximum women do not have job satisfaction. Maximum women do not want to take it as their career. The tendency to leave the job is indicating the higher level injustice happens in the career of sales girls in Bangladesh.

References:

American Heritage Dictionary of the English Language, 4th ed (2009). Houghton Mifflin Company.

Adidam, Phani T. (2006) *"Causes and Consequences of High Turnover by Sales Professionals,"* Journal of American Academy of Business, Cambridge.

Asian Development Bank (2008) *"Informal Employment in Bangladesh"* working paper.

Avila, R. (1988) "Unraveling Criteria for Assessing the Performance of Salespeople: A Causal Analysis," Journal of Personal Selling and Sales Management.

Argo, J. and Katherine, W. (2011) *"When Do Consumers Eat More? The Role of Appearance Self-Esteem and Food Packaging Cues,"* forthcoming at the *Journal of Marketing.*

Beneria, L. (2001) "Gender, development, and globalization: economics as if all people mattered," Routledge publisher.

Bensiman, E. and Marshall, C. (1997) "Policy analysis for post-secondary education. Feminist and critical perspectives" London, Falmer Press.

Butler, J. (1990) *"Gender trouble: Feminism and the subversion of identity"* Routledge, New York.

Charmes, J. (2000) *"Informal Sector, Poverty and Gender: A review of empirical study"* Background paper for the world development report 2001.Washington DC.

Cain, Khanam and Nahar. (1979) *"Class, Patriarchy and Women,s Work in Bangladesh"* Population and Development Review, Vol 5(3) pp.405-38.

Chen, M.A. (2001) *"Women in the informal sector: a global picture, the global movement",* SAIS *Review.*

Chen, M.A. and Lund (2002) *"Supporting workers in the informal economy: a policy framework"*, ILO Employment Sector Working Paper on the Informal Economy.

Chen, M. (2006) *"Informality, Gender and Poverty: A Global Picture,"* Economic and Political Weekly.

Comer (2003) *"The impact of realistic job previews and perceptions of training on sales force performance and continuance commitment: a longitudinal test,"* Journal of Personal Selling & Sales Management.

Comer, L.;Jolson, A.;Dubinsky and Yammarino, F (1995) *"When the Sales Manager Is a Woman: An Exploration Into the Relationship Between Salespeople's Gender and Their Responses to Leadership Style"* Journal of Personal Selling and Sales Management.

Dawson, L. M. (1997) *"Ethical Differences between Men and Women in the Sales Profession"* Journal of Business Ethics , Vol. 16.

Dubas, K. and L. Hershey (2007) *"The Optimal Rate of Sales Force Turnover,"* Proceedings of the Academy of Marketing Studies.

Devine, M. and Clutterbuck, D. (1987) *"Paradoxes of Globalization, Liberalization and Gender Equality: The Worldviews of the Lower Middle Classes in West Bengal"* in Gender and Society, Vol. 17.

Dorothy, S. (1987) *"The everyday world as a problematic: A feminist sociology"* Toronto, The University press of Toronto.

Feldman, S. (1992) *"Crisis, Islam and Gender in Bangladesh: The Social Construction of a Female Labor Force"*. In L. Beneria and S. Feldman (eds.) Unequal Burden: Economic crises, persistent poverty and Women's work.

Gerhart, B., & Rynes, S. (1991) *"Determinants and consequences of salary negotiations by male and female MBA graduates"* Journal of Applied Psychology.

Giuffre, W. and Patti A. and Christine L. (1994) *"Boundary Lines: Sexual Harassment in Restaurants"* Gender & Society vol 8.

Hart, K. (1973) *"Informal Income Opportunities and Urban Employment in Ghana"*, Journal of Modern African Studies,11(1),

Harding, S. (2005*) "New Feminist Approaches to Social Science Methodologies"* serial publication.

Hanson, S. and Pratt, G.(1995) "Gender, work, and space) Routledge, London ; New York.
Hartmann, Mitchell (1981, 1976; 1974, 1971) *"Salesmen, Saleswomen, or Sales Workers? Determinants of the Sex Composition of Sales Occupations,"* Springers press.

International Labour Office (ILO) (2003) :*Equality, Labour and Social Protection for Women and Men in the Formal and Informal Economy in VietNam: Issues for Advocacy and Policy Development"* Geneva, International Labour Office.

Joshi, M. (2007) *"Sexy salesgirls do actually boost sales"* Journal of Consumer Research.

Kandiyoti, D. (1998) *"Gender, Power and Consentation: Rethinking bargaining with Patriarchy"* Routledge, London, New York.

Khan, A. (2000) *"Experiences and Problems of Working Women as sales girls"* Thesis, Gender studies Quaid-e-Azam University, Islamabad.

Loscocco, K. and Spitze, G. (1991) *"The organizational context of women's and men's pay satisfaction"* journal of Social Science Quarterly.

Mohanty, C. (1991) "*Under Western Eyes: Feminist Scholarship and Colonial Discourses Third World Women and the Politics of Feminism"* Blooming: Indiana university Press.

Maria, C. and David, B. (2004) *"Occupational Ghettos: The Worldwide Segregation of Women and Men"* Stanford University press.

Mcdowell, L. and Pringle, R. (1992) *"Defining Women: Social Institutions and Gender Divisions"* Cambridge Polity Press.

Mackinnon (2002) *"Multiple, compound and intersectional discrimination: Bringing the experiences of the most marginalised to the fore"*

Neill, J. (2006) *"Analysis of Professional Literature: Qualitative Research,"* Retrieved

Putnam, D. (1988). *"Diplomacy and domestic politics: The logic of two-level games"* International Organization.

Romero, M. *(1992) "The Inclusion of Citizenship Status in* Intersectionality*"*, Routledge, Newyork.

Renard, M.K., (1992) *"Salary negotiations and the male-female wage gap."*, Unpublished Dissertation, University of Maryland.

Ransford, M. (1998) *"Women transforming sales into a female-dominated career"* Ball State University press.

Ransford, H. Eduard (1983) *''Race, Sex, and Feminist Outlooks,''* American Sociological Review.

Sarkar, S. (2007) *"Gender, Work and Poverty"*, Serials Publication, New Delhi.

Smith, D. (1981) *"Women, Class and Family"*, paper presented for SSHRC Workshop on Women and the Canadian Labor Force, U.B.C.

Sethuraman, S.V (1998) *"Gender, Informality and Poverty: A Global Review,"* World Bank, Washington, DC.

Siegle, D. (2010) *"Principles and Methods in Educational Research,"* Retrieved 05 01, from Web-Base html.

Safilios, R. (1974) *"Women and Social Policy"* Prentice Hall Press.

StevenS, C. (199) "Gender differences in the acquisition of salary negotiation skills: The role of goals, I self-efficacy, and perceived control" Journal of applied psychology,

QUESTIONNAIRE FOR SALES GIRL

1. Sex.

2. Age

3. Place of Residence

4. Marital Status

5. Educational Qualification

6. House type

7. Income

8. Family members

1. What is customer's behavior towards you? Is it positive or negative?

2. Mostly what type of customer visit your firm?

3. What is the difference between men's attitude and women's attitude when they negotiate?

4. Do you find harsh customers? How you deal with them?

5. Do you take help of a male counterpart or not?

6. Do you feel women's participation in sales profession is acceptable for customers?

7. What kind of issues you mostly face during your job in this firm?

8. Do you think that job environment of this firm is women friendly?

9. Do you feel women are well received by both men and women as sales managers?

10. Do you think that there is any kind of difference in women's and men's working abilities?

11. Do you feel working pressure under the male's supervision? Also clarify that why men are mostly on higher positions?

12. In your view why women are mostly hired on sales girls position?

13. Do you feel any difference in the behavior of different age customers?

14. What is the easiest and most difficult part of your job?

15. Do you feel women should come in this profession?

16. Do you think, this profession is respectable according to our societal norms?

17. What type of challenges usually you face?

18. What is your working experience?

QUESTIONNAIRE FOR SALES MEN

1. Sex.

2. Age

3. Place of Residence

4. Marital Status

5. Educational Qualification

6. House type

7. Income

8. Family members

1.   Do you feel this profession (sales) is suitable for women?

2.   Do you feel women are well received by both men and women as sales managers?

3.   Do you feel any difference between women's selling and men's selling?

4.   Do you feel women should come in this profession?

5.   Do you think, this profession is respectable according to our societal norms?

6. Do you feel sales men have upper hand and dominance when they work with saleswomen?

7. Do you feel that women are often haired at low level of job in sales profession?

8. Do you feel women are hard working than men?

9. Do you feel women have better skills in selling commodities?